HOLLYWOOD

THE INTERNET FOR KIDS

A TRUE BOOK

by
Charnan and
Tom Kazunas

Children's Press®
A Division of Grolier Publishing

New York   London   Hong Kong   Sydney
Danbury, Connecticut

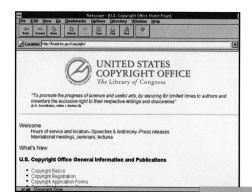

Reading Consultant
Linda Cornwell
Learning Resource Consultant
Indiana Department of
Education

To my parents, Angie and
Al, for their love and
support.

Find information about
the copyright system
on the Internet.

Library of Congress Cataloging-in-Publication Data

Kazunas, Charnan and Tom.
    The Internet for Kids / by Tom and Charnan Kazunas.
        p.   cm. — (A true book)
    Includes bibliographical references and index.
    Summary: A simple introduction to the Internet, the worldwide net-
work of computers that communicate with each other, and its many
uses.
    ISBN 0-516-20334-7 (lib. bdg.)   0-516-26170-3 (pbk.)
    1. Internet (Computer network)—Juvenile literature.   2.
Computers—Juvenile literature.   [1. Internet (Computer network). 2.
Computers.] I. Kazunas, Tom II. Series.
TK5105.875.I57K39 1997
004.67'8—dc21   96-49661
                                                                          CIP
                                                                          AC

Contents

Address: http://www.whitehouse.gov/WH/kids/html/TYCOTI.html

Dear Friends:

Welcome to the White House for Kids Home Page. President Clinton and I are pleased that you are participating in "Take Your Children on the Internet Week." With the help and guidance of their parents and teachers, children can find interesting and entertaining information on the Internet; adults and children alike can learn to enjoy and appreciate new computer technologies that are becoming increasingly important to life in the information age.

Here at the White House for Kids Home Page, for example, you can learn about the history of the White House, find out the President's favorite food, or send the President and me an e-mail message. By visiting the site of the GLOBE program (Global Learning and Observations to Benefit the Environment), you can discover a fascinating worldwide network of students, teachers, and scientists working together to study and understand the global environment. At other places on the Internet, you can make friends with a pen pal from another country, see famous paintings located at the Louvre museum in Paris, even dissect a frog -- all without leaving your classroom or your home.

The President and I believe that it is vitally important that all children be technologically literate as we enter the 21st century. We have challenged parents, teachers, business leaders and others to join us in a new national mission to make computers and learning devices accessible to every student; to

Vice President Gore encourages use of computers and the Internet.

Introduction

Vice President Al Gore declared the week of October 13, 1996 to be Take Your Children on the Internet Week. He wants children, with the help of their parents and teachers, "to enjoy and appreciate" all the new and exciting things the Internet has to offer.

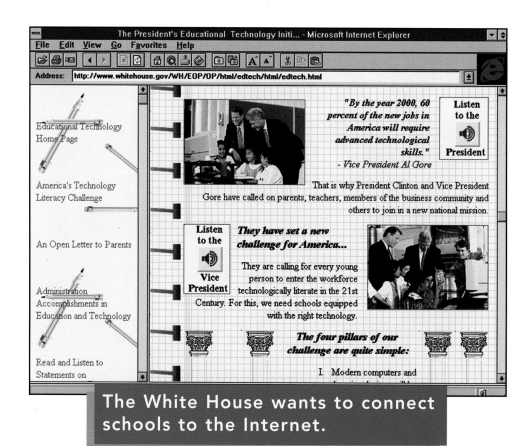

The White House wants to connect schools to the Internet.

Just what is the Internet and why is even the vice president of the United States so interested in it?

Networks

When two or more computers are connected to each other, they become a network. People who use networked computers can share information with each other, exchange messages, and even run the same programs at the same time on many different computers.

More schools have connected to the Internet.

Private networks let businesses, schools, and libraries connect all the computers in their buildings. Networks help factories keep track of their customers' orders. Networks make it easier for schools to record grades, keep attendance records, and plan lunch menus. Networks help people find the books they need when they visit the library.

Computer networks keep track of goods in a warehouse and books in a library.

The Internet

The Internet is like a private network, only much bigger. In fact, the Internet is made up of many different networks combined. Here's how the Internet got its start.

In 1980, a large group of scientists found themselves working on the same projects,

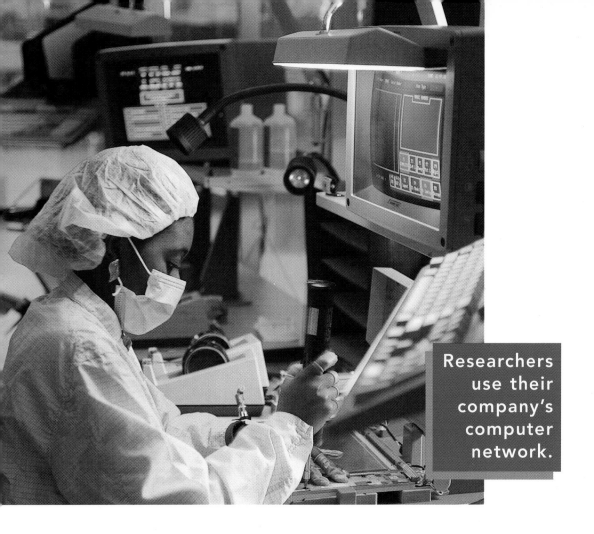

but from different parts of the United States. They needed a faster way to share information than sending messages through the mail. The scientists set up a special network that connected not only computers in one building, but computers around the world.

This world-wide network was called the Internet. Today the Internet is open to the public to explore. It connects more than sixty thousand networks, each with its own collection of articles, pictures, sounds, programs (such as games) and other information.

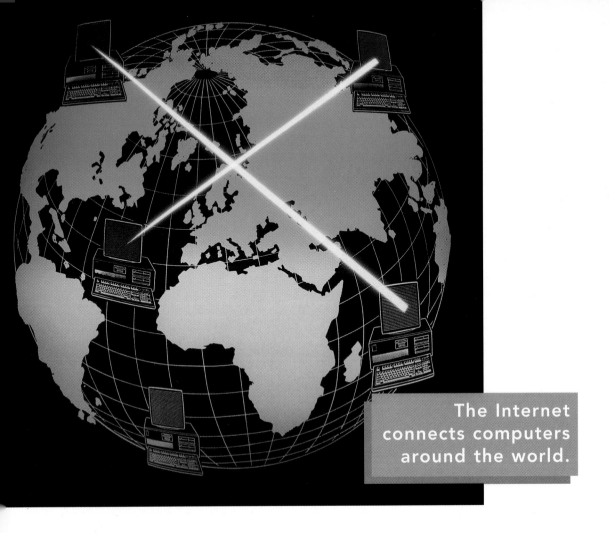

The Internet connects computers around the world.

Millions of Americans use their computers to communicate and share information through the Internet.

What's on the Internet?

Imagine you are writing a report on whales. You check out library books as usual, but this time you also use your computer to access the Internet. You might find articles on whale behavior, see photographs and diagrams of different whale species, or study maps of whale migration. You might watch movie clips of whales in action, or even examine 3D computer simulations of whales in motion.

When you're done, you can publish your work on the Internet too.

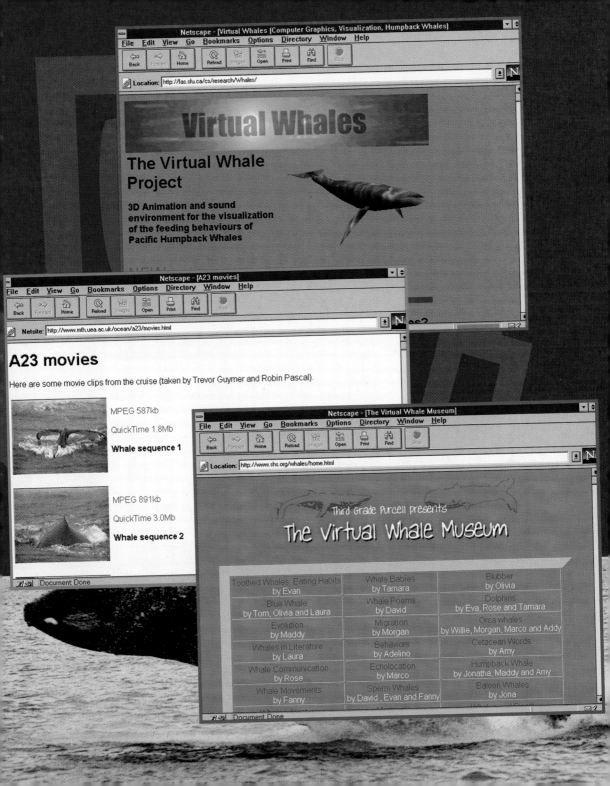

Netscape - [Virtual Whales [Computer Graphics, Visualization, Humpback Whales]]

File Edit View Go Bookmarks Options Directory Window Help

Back Forward Home Reload Images Open Print Find Stop

Location: http://fas.sfu.ca/cs/research/Whales/

Virtual Whales

The Virtual Whale Project

3D Animation and sound environment for the visualization of the feeding behaviours of Pacific Humpback Whales

---

Netscape - [A23 movies]

File Edit View Go Bookmarks Options Directory Window Help

Back Forward Home Reload Images Open Print Find Stop

Netsite: http://www.mth.uea.ac.uk/ocean/a23/movies.html

A23 movies

Here are some movie clips from the cruise (taken by Trevor Guymer and Robin Pascal).

MPEG 587kb

QuickTime 1.8Mb

Whale sequence 1

MPEG 891kb

QuickTime 3.0Mb

Whale sequence 2

Document Done

Netscape - [The Virtual Whale Museum]

File Edit View Go Bookmarks Options Directory Window Help

Back Forward Home Reload Images Open Print Find Stop

Location: http://www.shs.org/whales/home.html

Third Grade Purcell presents
The Virtual Whale Museum

Toothed Whales: Eating Habits by Evan	Whale Babies by Tamara	Blubber by Olivia
Blue Whale by Tom, Olivia and Laura	Whale Poems by David	Dolphins by Eva, Rose and Tamara
Evolution by Maddy	Migration by Morgan	Orca whales by Willie, Morgan, Marco and Addy
Whales in Literature by Laura	Behaviors by Adelino	Cetacean Words by Amy
Whale Communication by Rose	Echolocation by Marco	Humpback Whale by Jonatha, Maddy and Amy
Whale Movements by Fanny	Sperm Whales by David , Evan and Fanny	Baleen Whales by Jona

Document Done

How It All Works

Computers connected to each other form a network. Networks connected to each other form the Internet. But with all the information available on the Internet, how do you get to what you're looking for?

Each of the thousands of individual networks that make

16

Servers like the one on the right serve information like a waitress serves food.

up the Internet has set aside one or more computers to act as a server. These computer servers play host to Internet sites, and serve their information to computer users the way a waiter serves food in a restaurant. And, like a restaurant, each of these servers has its own address. Servers keep track of the addresses of all of the other servers on the Internet, and what sites you will find on them. In a way, every server has a menu—a very long and detailed menu—of all the other servers on the Internet.

Connecting to the Internet

All of these computers and computer networks are connected to each other through telephone lines. That's where the term "on-line" comes from. You can connect your own computer to the Internet using a telephone line, the right software, and a subscription to either an Internet provider or an online service.

Internet providers give you access to all the networks on the Internet. Online services, such as America Online or CompuServe, also provide access to the Internet. In addition, they let you play games and use information that you can't get on the Internet.

To find a site on the Internet, you first connect your computer to an Internet server. This server is owned by your Internet provider. When you direct your computer to a particular Internet site, your Internet software will ask this first server to find that site.

Then one server will pass your request on to another and to another, until the address is reached.

Internet Addresses

Internet addresses are called URLs (Uniform Resource Locators). Some look long and confusing, while others are quite short, but they all follow the same simple rules.

The first group of letters on every address tells the network which protocol to use.

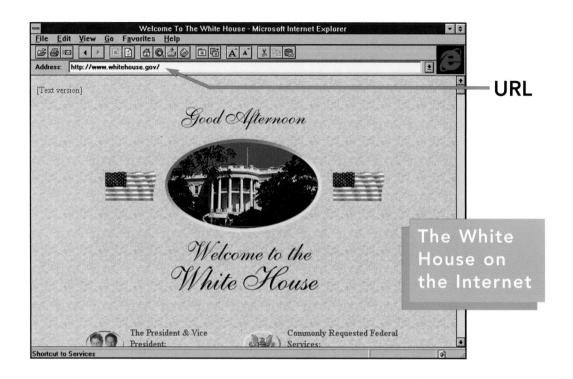

URL

[Text version]

Good Afternoon

Welcome to the
White House

The White
House on
the Internet

The President & Vice
President:

Commonly Requested Federal
Services:

Shortcut to Services

A protocol is like a language—
you have to know which one
to speak. One common protocol is **http**, which stands for
HyperText Transport Protocol.
The protocol is followed by a
colon and two slashes (://).

Next comes the domain name. Domain names contain at least two words or phrases, separated by periods. An example would be

www.whitehouse.gov

• **www** means the site is on the World Wide Web.

• **whitehouse** points to a specific server, in this case the server at the White House in Washington, DC.

• the word on the right tells you what kind of site you are visiting. In this example, the address has something to do with the government (that's what "gov" stands for).

To visit the White House server and read Vice President Gore's Internet message for yourself, put all the pieces together and enter **http://www.whitehouse.gov.**

The Parts of the Internet

The Internet has several different parts: electronic or e-mail, the World Wide Web, chat sessions, Telnet, and USENET Newsgroups are some of the most popular. Each part has a special purpose and way of working.

Write letters and send them through the mail (right). Write e-mail and send it through the Internet (below).

Netscape - [Message Composition]

File **Edit** **View** **Options** **Window**

Send   Quote   Attach   Address   Stop

Mail To: Mark

Cc:

Subject: True Books

Attachment:

Hi Mark,

Have you seen the latest True Books? They are excellent!

Your friend,

Allison

E-mail is the simplest use of the Internet. With e-mail you can write an electronic letter on your computer, and send it to another person almost instantly, even if that person in halfway around the world. You can also attach pictures or sounds to an e-mail message.

How does the message get where it is going? An e-mail address is a kind of electronic mail box set up on an Internet server.

Internet Safety

There are a few safety rules that you should follow when surfing the Net (that's what you call exploring the Internet). Never give your name, address or phone number to people you don't know. If you are uncomfortable with anything you see or read while on-line, tell your parents immediately.

America Online

File   Edit   Go To   Mail   Members   Window   Help

KO Chat – Safety Tips

AOL Kids Only   **Safety Tips**

1 Don't give your AOL password to anyone, even your best friend.

Never tell someone your home address, telephone number, or school name without asking a parent. **2**

3 Never say you will meet someone in person without asking a parent.

Always tell a parent about any threatening or bad language you see online. **4**

5 If someone says something that makes you feel unsafe or funny, don't just sit there - take charge! Call a Guide (keyword KO Help), leave the chat room, or just sign off.

create

sports

stars

Fun-ergize the ABC Ki

hot

Go Chat!

Welcome, Pipiciayon!

SafeSurf Home Page - Microso

File   Edit   View   Go   Favorites   Help

Address: http://www.safesurf.com/

The Original Interne

Update Explorer

Rate Your Site

Rating System Explained

Welcome to
Saf
HomePage

Join us

Help us

Kid's Wave

Internet Lifeguard

S.E.R.F Page

The new generation is here:
SafeSurf Internet Filtering Solution™
for Libraries, Schools, Businesses and ISPs.

Press Releases

Awards Received

CyberAngels

Entertainment Monitor

NEW! Update Microsoft's Internet Explorer to support SafeSurf Ratings.

Help us achieve a safe and free Internet. We've designed a special form to help you rate your Web site.

We're an organization dedicated to making the Internet safe for your children without censorship. We've developed and are implementing an Internet Rating Standard that is bringing together parents

And did you know that computers can catch viruses just like humans? These viruses are a kind of computer program, not a real disease. Ask an adult to check any programs you retrieve from the Internet with "virus detection" software before you use them.

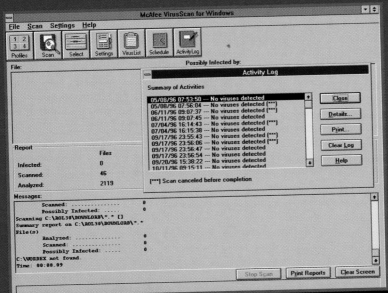

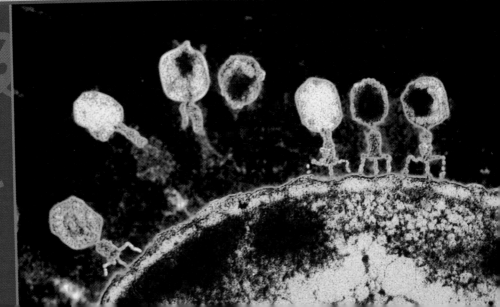

E-mail addresses look like this: **jsmith@aol.com**. In this example, "jsmith" is the name of the person who gets the letter. The name is followed by an "at" sign (@), which tells the network that a server name is coming next. In this case "aol.com" is the address for America Online.

The World Wide Web is the newest part of the Internet, and the most popular. The Web brings color,

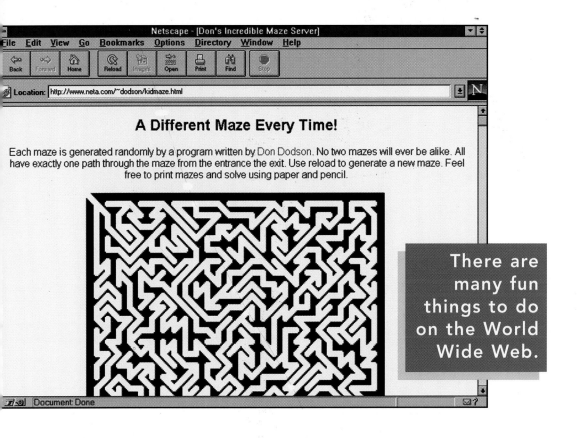

File   Edit   View   Go   Bookmarks   Options   Directory   Window   Help

Back   Forward   Home   Reload   Images   Open   Print   Find   Stop

Location: http://www.neta.com/~dodson/kidmaze.html

A Different Maze Every Time!

Each maze is generated randomly by a program written by Don Dodson. No two mazes will ever be alike. All have exactly one path through the maze from the entrance the exit. Use reload to generate a new maze. Feel free to print mazes and solve using paper and pencil.

Document Done

> There are many fun things to do on the World Wide Web.

moving pictures and sound to your computer screen. When you're done looking at one Web page, click on a short-cut called a hyperlink to whisk off to other Web pages.

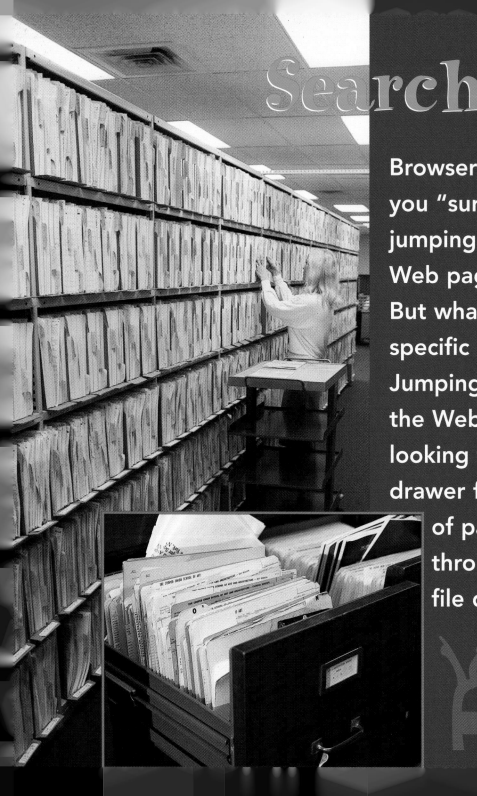

Search an

Browser software le
you "surf the Net"
jumping from one
Web page to anoth
But what if you nee
specific information
Jumping around on
the Web can be like
looking through a fi
drawer for one shee
of paper—or
through many
file drawers.

Retrieval Tools

Fortunately, there are many "search engine" sites and indexes on the Web to help you find information.

Gopher software also searches and retrieves files across the entire Internet with typed commands. Gophers may not be pretty to look at, but they retrieve information fast.

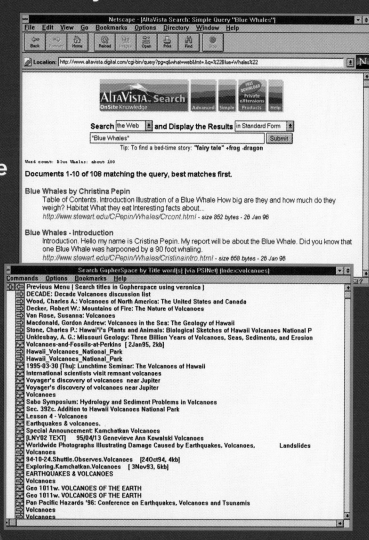

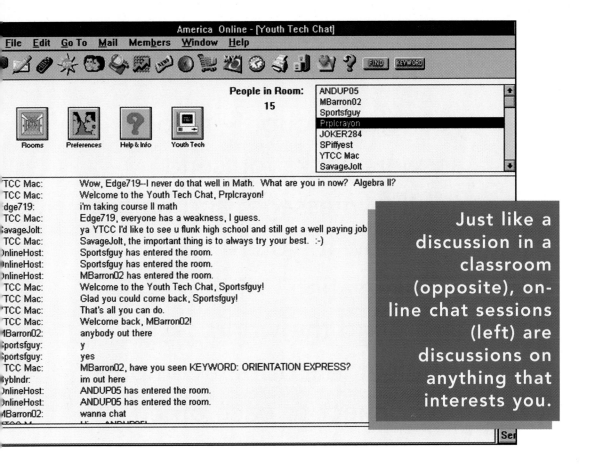

America Online - [Youth Tech Chat]

File   Edit   Go To   Mail   Members   Window   Help

Rooms	Preferences	Help & Info	Youth Tech

People in Room:
15

ANDUP05
MBarron02
Sportsfguy
Prplcrayon
JOKER284
SPiffyest
YTCC Mac
SavageJolt

TCC Mac: Wow, Edge719--I never do that well in Math. What are you in now? Algebra II?
TCC Mac: Welcome to the Youth Tech Chat, Prplcrayon!
dge719:   i'm taking course II math
TCC Mac: Edge719, everyone has a weakness, I guess.
SavageJolt: ya YTCC I'd like to see u flunk high school and still get a well paying job
TCC Mac: SavageJolt, the important thing is to always try your best. :-)
OnlineHost: Sportsfguy has entered the room.
OnlineHost: Sportsfguy has entered the room.
OnlineHost: MBarron02 has entered the room.
TCC Mac: Welcome to the Youth Tech Chat, Sportsfguy!
TCC Mac: Glad you could come back, Sportsfguy!
TCC Mac: That's all you can do.
TCC Mac: Welcome back, MBarron02!
MBarron02:   anybody out there
Sportsfguy: y
Sportsfguy: yes
TCC Mac: MBarron02, have you seen KEYWORD: ORIENTATION EXPRESS?
yblndr: im out here
OnlineHost: ANDUP05 has entered the room.
OnlineHost: ANDUP05 has entered the room.
MBarron02:   wanna chat

Just like a discussion in a classroom (opposite), on-line chat sessions (left) are discussions on anything that interests you.

Chat sessions let you "talk" to people all over the world. You type in a message and instantly it is sent to all the other people tuned into your chat group. Someone answers back, you send another message, and before you know it, you're having a "conversation" with people all around the world.

Telnet lets distant computers connect to each other and run each other's programs. If your public library uses Telnet, you can hook your computer into the library's system to find and reserve the book you want.

With Telnet, you can use a library's catalog in your home.

Newsgroups are like magazines— there's one for every interest.

USENET Newsgroups are electronic discussion groups. In such a group, people around the world "discuss" a subject, like in a chat session. Only, instead of talking at the same time, members of a newsgroup post messages on electronic bulletin boards. Anyone "subscribing" to the newsgroup can then read these messages and leave their own message in reply.

For example, if you and your friends like Dalmatian puppies, you could set up a newsgroup for everyone who likes Dalmatians—if there isn't one already. You can then share your knowledge and questions all around the world. Eventually, thousands of people might subscribe.

The Future of the Internet

The Internet is getting busier every day. But as thousands of new users log on each month, the Internet is also getting slower.

To keep from slowing down completely, the Internet of the future will probably be split up into

41

several different networks. Users might choose from several Internet channels. Cable TV companies are working on ways to use their cables and satellites to connect your computer to the Internet— and your TV and telephone, as well.

One day you might get news and shows from Internet boxes, instead of newspapers and television. You'll order groceries from

Newspapers and television networks are already moving onto the Internet.

your TV. And Vice President Gore's next Internet message might be delivered right to your family Internet phone.

To Find Out More

Here are some additional resources to help you learn more about personal computers:

 **Books**

 **Internet Sites**

Brimner, Larry Dane. **The World Wide Web.** Children's Press, 1997.

Gralla, Preston. **On-Line Kids: A Young Surfer's Guide to Cyberspace.** John Wiley & Sons, 1996.

Pedersen, Ted, and Francis Moss. **Internet for Kids: A Beginner's Guide to Surfing the Net.** Price Stern Sloan, 1995.

Salzman, Marian, and Robert Pondisco. **Kids On-Line.** Avon Books, 1995.

Just for Kids, A Page of Fun Stuff Just for Kids *http://www.alaska.net/ ~steel/kidsfun.html*

Suggested Internet sites to explore topics like "Animal Stuff," "Comics," "Games," "Movies," and even "Things That Go."

Sea World/Busch Gardens Animal Information Database *http://www.bev.net/ education/SeaWorld*

Find information on aardvarks to zebras, and test your knowledge with fun quizzes.

Seussville

http://www.randomhouse.com/seussville/

This is the official Dr. Seuss site, with quizzes, contests, activities, and an "Ask the Cat-in-the-Hat" feature.

Smithsonian FTP site

ftp://photo1.si.edu/images/gif89a/science-nature

Animal pictures in GIF format, free for educational use.

The White House

http://www.whitehouse.gov

Let Socks the White House cat guide you through the most famous residence in the world. A look at its occupants as well as the building.

Yahooligans

http://www.yahooligans.com

The best place to begin a search for kid stuff on the net.

Important Words

browser a program used to look at Wide World Web pages on the Internet

hypertext words or phrases in an Internet document that connect to another document

network a collection of computers that share information and programs

protocol a set of rules computers follow to communicate and share information

server a computer and software that manages the flow of information on a computer network

URL Universal Resource Locator; the address of a World Wide Web page

World Wide Web the part of the Internet using graphics and hypertext

Index

(**Boldface** page numbers indicate illustrations.)

Meet the Author

Charnan Simon and Tom Kazunas are married and live in Madison, Wisconsin, with their daughters, Ariel and Hana, their dog Sam, and their two computers.

Tom's computer is new and fast and powerful. Tom uses it to solve complicated math problems, design books, visit websites, do research, and play all kinds of games.

Charnan's computer is old and slow and tired. Every morning when she turns it on, it says "Disk boot failure." This means Charnan has time to walk the dog, make a cup of tea, and write a postcard to a friend. By then her computer is warmed up, and Charnan can get to work writing books.